New Day

FRESH START

All contributions by Naomi Grant, Jessica Koulianos, Julianna Morlet, Rhoda Turner, and Lauralyn Vasquez are used by permission of the authors.

New Day Fresh Start
© 2015 Brandie Manigault. All rights reserved.
ISBN: 978-0692426166

DEDICATION

To my Grandmothers

Constance Jones and Evelyn Reynolds

Two women whose strength inspires me, whose

love encourages me, and whose shoulders I stand.

CONTENTS

FOREWORD

When we come to the realization that we can't do it all and there is more balance to life than we are currently experiencing, it's important that we make the decision to separate ourselves for the purpose of drawing all we can from God and His word. Each day we find ourselves juggling more than we can physically handle, and at the end of the day we collapse into bed from spiritual, mental or physical exhaustion. God never intended for life to be this way; instead He desires for His divine grace to be in operation in our lives. When we choose to feed on God's word grace manifests and that grace provides everything we need to accomplish any task set before us. Through grace and God's Word life becomes manageable, and transformation inevitable.

New Day Fresh Start embodies what women all over the world need, and that's a revelation from God's Word that they have the power and ability to do and be all that God has called for. Knowing Brandie Manigault from her youth, I can honestly say that she is a living-breathing example of such a woman. While tending to her marriage, ministry, children, and home God is using her to effect change in the lives of many. Her message is practical and her ministry powerful. I believe any woman reading New Day Fresh Start will be blessed as they allow Him to be all He desires to be in their life.

God bless you!

Melva L. Henderson
Founder/Pastor
World Outreach & Bible Training Center
Glendale, WI

MY WHY

New Day Fresh Start is all about changing your day. I learned, through trial and error, that how I start my day is very important; usually dictating my attitude and my actions. If I woke up flustered, I usually felt rushed for the rest of the day. If I started out on the "wrong side of the bed", I would usually spend the day challenged by my attitude, but if I woke up peaceful and determined to have a good day, then that's exactly what I had.

I heard a pastor-friend preach one day about us (individuals) being "transformers". In a nutshell the pastor said, "If you don't like the climate around you, if your atmosphere isn't what you want it to be then change it." How profound!

I initially started writing these daily motivations to encourage myself. Having a husband with a demanding schedule, three children with even more demanding schedules, and then trying to manage my own personal schedule, I started becoming frustrated with my commitment to reading my

Bible. I hated the fact that I couldn't sit down and read chapter after chapter, or even a chapter like others some days, and if I did I wasn't retaining most of it because I was so tired. I know. I know. I shouldn't compare myself to others, but I did anyway- don't judge me!

So one day I committed to the Lord that I was going to get up at 6:30am before everyone else got up, and I was going to read. Well, I'm not a morning person (especially when the night is filled with random visits from my children because they can't sleep, or they just want to get in my bed for no reason at all), so that extra half of an hour was definitely a sacrifice, but it quickly made all the difference.

With a new motivation I picked up my Bible at 6:30am one morning and started reading. But it had to be more than that for me; it had to be more than just a good read, something I checked off my to-do list for the day. So I decided to challenge myself further. I wanted to see how I could apply the life of Jesus more to my life. I figured what better place to start than the Book of Matthew to learn about the life of Jesus. If you want to be like Jesus, why not read about Jesus? So every day I read from Matthew until I finished it.

At that hour of the morning, in all honesty, I really could only read and meditate on a couple of Scriptures at a time. So that's what I did. I read those few Scriptures and then spent a few minutes thinking about what it meant and how I could apply something from it to my own life. Then I purposed to try it. Whatever I got from those Scriptures was going to be my focus for the day. I challenged myself to let that inspire or shape my attitude, how I treated others, and what I thought about myself.

And it worked. My day was more focused. I treated people better. I had more patience with my husband and my children. Additionally, I didn't feel self-condemned about not reading chapter and chapter. I didn't feel like I was "disappointing" God, because I hadn't prioritized my time in His word. Let me say this… I know ultimately God didn't view me as a failure because of my lack of time in His word, neither did He condemn me, but my love for Him left me wanting to be with Him more and prioritize my time with Him. I knew it was a gift that He would love and that I would greatly benefit from. This season of my life just didn't allow for that every day, and that's OK. Seasons change. Previous seasons allowed for it; this one didn't. He knew my schedule and what I could and could not do, but this, this was something I could do. One Scripture a day at the top of my day was something manageable for me. Now there were days when I did have the time to dive into the Word and spend more time, but by and large, my days were pretty packed Monday through Friday and on the weekends (smile).

What started out as personal mission to get my day right has grown; the passion I had for my own daily success grew into a passion to encourage others (you).

So my prayer as I write each motivation is that the power of God's Word would jump off the page and become alive in each of our hearts (mine included), that His Words would ultimately help us to love Him more, ourselves more, and others more by its transforming power, and that it would challenge and change us to be better and to do better.

I asked a few friends of mine to come along on this journey and share with you their experiences from the book of Matthew. The writings of Naomi Grant, Jessica Koulianos, Julianna Morlet, Rhoda Turner, and Lauralyn Vasquez will inspire you and challenge you to make the most of your day.

As you take this journey to transform your day, I pray that you also take the time to enjoy it, maximize your day. It's not a day that you've seen before and one that you won't see again. Why not make it count?

In the back of the book there are blank pages for you to help document this journey. When you begin reading this book write down your thoughts, your challenges, what you want to see happen over the course of this read. Then at the end write down your observations of where the journey has taken you, how you feel, and what has changed.

I believe in you. Let the journey begin!

-Brandie

New Day
FRESH START

1

Did you know that where we come from doesn't matter to God? Our family history may contain drug addicts, prostitutes, felons, do-gooders, overachievers, workaholics, Muslims, Jews, and Christians. Our family may look like a melting pot of all things or we can come from a strong lineage of Jesus lovers, but none of those things matter. When the Lord of all creation chose us, He made a decision based on us individually. He did not qualify us based on what our family looked like or their history. He can and will use us individually in spite of all those things; the good and the bad.

Challenge

Today challenge yourself to stop disqualifying yourself based on how you look on paper. Be open and willing to be used by God, and let that be the only thing on your resume.

Matthew 1:16, *v.1-15

And Jacob begot Joseph the husband of Mary,

of whom was born Jesus who is called Christ.

2

What's inside of you is so much more than you could have ever imagined. It's easy to think that we are pregnant with a dream just to make us happy. We think that burning desire on the inside is just so that we can prosper financially. We assumed that we were pursuing a particular career path out of obedience to someone in authority. Boy are we wrong! We are pregnant with the possibility to change the world. It goes beyond us and our own houses. It reaches the nations. He has trusted us with a seed, a gift, a dream, and a passion so that His plan would be fulfilled in the earth. Our circumstances may not be ideal, but that should not discourage us. We cannot abort. We must carry until it's time to push, push when we feel the contractions, and then deliver when the time is right.

Challenge

Today challenge yourself to be an agent of change. No matter what it looks like around you, know that you are making a difference.

Matthew 1:20-21

And she will bring forth a Son, and you shall call His name Jesus, for He will save His people from their sins."

3

So now what? We have stepped out in faith and in obedience to the Word of the Lord and have now given birth to our promise. So now what? We are holding in our arms a miracle. No one thought it was possible. We even had doubts of our own at times, but now it's here... the business we've always wanted to start, the book we wanted to write, the degree we studied for. So now what? What we once hid on the inside for protection is now out in the open for people to see. So now what? Now we wait for the supernatural provision of the Lord. He has announced the birth of our baby and people are headed our way with the supplies needed to propel us forward. He knows that we cannot do it alone.

Challenge

Today, challenge yourself to sit and be patient. Don't try to make things happen on your own. Provision is coming. Just wait on it.

Matthew 2:11

And when they had come into the house, they saw the young Child with Mary His mother, and fell down and worshiped Him. And when they had opened their treasures, they presented gifts to Him: gold, frankincense, and myrrh.

4

There will always be something about you that makes you stand out in a crowd; your passion; your drive; your ability to be sensitive to the Holy Spirit. When God's hand is on you it will be hard to fit in, and because of that sometimes the Lord will have you in what seems like a foreign land so that you are protected until the appointed time of your reveal. Foreign places can often feel uncomfortable because they are different and unfamiliar, but don't be discouraged if you feel like you are in a land not your home. You are just being hidden for your safety. The time will come for you to come out of "hiding" and when it does, you will be in a place that welcomes you and receives you for who you are.

Challenge

Today, challenge yourself to thank God for hiding you and keeping you safe. Only He really knows the heart of those who you are surrounded by.

Matthew 2:13, 16, 22

Now when they had departed, behold, an angel of the Lord appeared to Joseph in a dream, saying, "Arise, take the young Child and His mother, flee to Egypt, and stay there until I bring you word; for Herod will seek the young Child to destroy Him." Then Herod, when he saw that he was deceived by the wise men, was exceedingly angry; and he sent forth and put to death all the male children who were in Bethlehem and in all its districts, from two years old and under, according to the time which he had determined from the wise men. But when he heard that Archelaus was reigning over Judea instead of his father Herod, he was afraid to go there. And being warned by God in a dream, he turned aside into the region of Galilee.

5

Our outward expressions are a reflection of our inward transformation. When we commit to changing our lives it has to be a complete package. We cannot just change our clothes and think we are new people. We must produce fruit that reflects the inward change. It doesn't matter how many good things we do as an outward gesture of transformation if we still have a bad attitude, still curse people out, or still judge them. Mentioning the name of someone who does good things will not help either. We cannot ride on the coattails of others who have a reputation of good fruit. It's something we have to do and produce for ourselves.

Challenge
Today challenge yourself. Keep a watchful eye on your fruit. Is it good fruit or is it rotten? And then adjust things according.

Matthew 3:7-10 (MSG)
..."Brood of snakes! What do you think you're

doing slithering down here to the river? Do you think a little water on your snakeskins is going to make any difference? It's your life that must change, not your skin! And don't think you can pull rank by claiming Abraham as father. Being a descendant of Abraham is neither here nor there. Descendants of Abraham are a dime a dozen. What counts is your life. Is it green and blossoming? Because if it's deadwood, it goes on the fire.

6

Stay in your lane. When you have been given an assignment by God you are also given authority to carry out that assignment along with the necessary instructions and tools for success. The problem comes when you look at your assignment and think of it as insignificant or even too much for you, so you assign yourself a different task. You have now switched into a lane that is not yours and this unauthorized switch has the potential to harm you and those around you. Others cannot do their job effectively because you are in the way, and you cannot do your job because you are not in the right place.

Challenge
Today challenge yourself to fully commit to your assignment and be at peace with it. Know that you have everything you need to carry out your task and then go for it.

Matthew 3:11

I indeed baptize you with water unto repentance, but He who is coming after me is mightier than I, whose sandals I am not worthy to carry. He will baptize you with the Holy Spirit and fire.

7

There is power in knowing the Word. It's not all about being able to quote Scripture and verse and translating it into Greek and Hebrew. When Jesus was being tempted by the devil He did not say, "Isaiah chapter 1 verses 1-3 says xyz". He told Satan what that verse said and let the power of the Scriptures work in His situation. He knew His word. It was inside of Him and He understood how to apply it. It's the same with us. When we say what the Bible says, it will work in our lives as well. The Word will turn our circumstances around. We just have to apply it.

Challenge
Today be confident in your knowledge of the Scriptures. Don't be afraid to say what the Bible says even if you can't say where it's found.

Matthew 4:4, 7, 10-11
…But He answered and said, "It is written, 'Man shall not live by bread alone, but by

every word that proceeds from the mouth of God.' " Jesus said to him, "It is written again, 'You shall not tempt the Lord your God.' " Then Jesus said to him, "Away with you, Satan! For it is written, 'You shall worship the Lord your God, and Him only you shall serve.' " Then the devil left Him, and behold, angels came and ministered to Him.

8

Do you know the power of your "YES"? One "YES" in obedience to the Lord will set off a chain of events that years of labor could not produce. The possibilities and the power of your "YES" are limitless. It puts things into motion. Your act of obedience today in taking a job offer you may feel over qualified for can lead to your promotion in the company and eventually you taking over. Your yes to sow a seed into someone's life could keep them from foreclosing on their home and ending up homeless, they remember you when they get on their feet, and leave you an inheritance later in life. There are potential outcomes to you saying "YES" to the Lord that you cannot imagine.

Challenge

Today challenge yourself to set off a chain reaction for your future; tell the Lord YES.

Matthew 4:18-20

And Jesus, walking by the Sea of Galilee, saw two brothers, Simon called Peter, and Andrew his brother, casting a net into the sea; for they were fishermen. Then He said to them, "Follow Me, and I will make you fishers of men." They immediately left their nets and followed Him.

Matthew 16:18

And I also say to you that you are Peter, and on this rock I will build My church, and the gates of Hades shall not prevail against it.

9

Do you know that atmospheres change when you enter a room without you having to do anything or even say one word? When you go to work, school, or the grocery store the darkness that exists in those places has to move when you arrive. Christ in you shines through you instantly turning dark places bright. You carry an unchallengeable light within you. You are supposed to make places better just by your presence alone. When the light of Christ shines through you it will illuminate and highlight things that have been hidden in the darkness and make vibrant colors that have been dimmed stand out even more.

Challenge

Today challenge yourself to challenge the darkness. Don't hold back. Be an example of Christ and shine bright!

Matthew 5:14-16 (MSG)

"Here's another way to put it: You're here to

be light, bringing out the God-colors in the world. God is not a secret to be kept. We're going public with this, as public as a city on a hill. If I make you light-bearers, you don't think I'm going to hide you under a bucket, do you? I'm putting you on a light stand. Now that I've put you there on a hilltop, on a light stand—shine!

10

We are called to make an impact in this world. We are not supposed to blend in and become part of the norm, but we are supposed to do and be the exact opposite; different. Our job is to be an asset in our families, at our schools, and at our jobs. These places should be bland without us around, lacking flavor and direction. It's our job to be us so boldly that when we are not around these areas feel our absence. It's important that we remember that we do not live these bold lives for our own benefit. The void they must feel when we are not around is the presence of God. Everything we say and everything we do must point to Him. When they look at us they must be able to see Christ in us.

Challenge

Today challenge yourself to be the difference that your job, school, or home needs. Give them Jesus with your presence.

Matthew 5:13-16

"You are the salt of the earth; but if the salt loses its flavor, how shall it be seasoned? It is then good for nothing but to be thrown out and trampled underfoot by men. "You are the light of the world. A city that is set on a hill cannot be hidden. Nor do they light a lamp and put it under a basket, but on a lampstand, and it gives light to all who are in the house. Let your light so shine before men, that they may see your good works and glorify your Father in heaven.

11

Repentance
Jessica Koulianos

Matthew 3:2 (NLT): "Repent of your sins and turn to God, for the Kingdom of Heaven is near."

Nowadays we rarely hear the word repent. It seems as taboo in the church as a four letter word. This, in my opinion, is one of the greatest tragedies the church faces today. **If we don't see the need of repentance, we lose appreciation of the beautiful suffering of the Cross.** We are all sinners and are in desperate need of a Savior. Repenting helps us realize how deeply we need Him and how deeply He loves us; enough to have laid down His life for our sins.

As the bride of Christ He deserves for us to ask for forgiveness when we have wronged Him. **We are in a covenant relationship with**

Him. Just as any spouse deserves an apology when they are hurt or forgotten, Christ also deserves that from us, His bride.

When I came back to the Lord I repented of my sins first. It didn't seem right to start this journey with Him and not ask Him to forgive my sins. I knew my sins hurt Him. I knew the life I lived was wrong, and I wanted Jesus to know that I was sorry. **I wanted to feel brand new and cleansed, and the only way I could feel that way was to humble myself and cry out to The Lord telling Him I was sorry for ever hurting Him.** It doesn't mean I don't fall short daily. I do all the time, and when I do, I humble myself before the Lord asking for His forgiveness and help on this journey we call the Christian life.

Without repentance, Jesus' dying for you and me on the Cross was done in vain, and His death is too precious to me to treat it that way.

Maybe it's been a long time since you sat down and just poured out your heart to the

Lord and repented of your sins or maybe you have never done this; I encourage you today to go before the Lord, [who would of died on the cross just for your sins alone], and ask Him to wash you clean and forgive you for any sins you have committed. Ask the Holy Spirit to show you where you are weak and to help you to live a life that is pleasing to God. **He is such a loving Father and quick to forgive His children.**

12

Loving Your Enemies
Lauralyn Vasquez

I'm not good at loving my enemy. In fact, I sometimes enjoy hating my enemy. There I said it. **So often I look around church or my community and wonder, "Am I the only Christ follower who does not like it when Jesus says "love your enemy?"** "Am I the only Christ-follower who sometimes wants to stick my tongue out at those who I do not like?" It has taken me years of wrestling to come to terms with this verse. There are all kinds of people who have wronged me; not one is as painful as my adopted Dad who physically abused my mom, my siblings and me. But after a while I started to understand that **my hatred towards my Dad was only hurting me**. He was off on his merry way enjoying life, on vacations and full of smiles while I was stewing, having conversations in my mind with him and angry.

Then one day my eyes were opened. One day I realized that Christ died for him as well as me. I was becoming a Pharisee and judge of the living. In the mean **time I was carrying around a huge burden of un-forgiveness, and it was keeping me from becoming more like Christ.** But how was I to love my enemy? That day I started writing down everything about my enemy that was in the image of Christ. See, he too was created in the image of God. He too needed Jesus. It was not up to me to share the gospel and be in a relationship with him, but it was for me to love my enemy, which meant, pray for him. **When I loved my enemy all of a sudden I loved me. All of a sudden, years of pain left me.**

Matthew 5:43-44 says, "You have heard that it was said, "love your neighbor and hate your enemy. But I tell you, love your enemies and pray for those who persecute you." I encourage to you identify who your enemy is and begin asking the questions: "How can I love them?" and "What about them is in the image of God?" Then commit to praying for those who persecute you.

13

There is just something to be said about possessing a trustworthy characteristic. There is something about being able to take someone at their word and them doing the same for us. Our word holds so much value that it will automatically validate or disqualify us in the eyes of others. We should be people of integrity, dependable people, people whose words mean something when said. When we say we are going to do something, there shouldn't be a doubt in the minds of others whether or not we will come through with what we said, because we have already weighed the cost before we committed. Others are depending on us to follow through on our commitments.

Challenge

Today challenge yourself to protect your reputation by doing what you say you are going to do. Your word is really all you have.

Matthew 5:37

But let your 'Yes' be 'Yes,' and your 'No,' 'No.' For whatever is more than these is from the evil one.

14

Have you ever been at a loss for words in prayer; you know you need to pray but you don't know what to pray? Have you ever been so emotionally full that all you have is silence and tears? These are the times when you can't even explain to other people what you are feeling and experiencing in order to have them pray for you. It is just you and the Father. What do you do? You pray like Jesus said to pray: "Your kingdom come. Your will be done on earth as it is in heaven." Put it in His hands and let Him figure out exactly what is needed in these moments on earth in your situation. He knows what it will take to make your situation better.

Challenge

Today challenge yourself to relinquish your need to conjure up the "right" words to pray, and use the prewritten script; it is much easier to use His words than to try and make up your own.

Matthew 6:9-10

In this manner, therefore, pray: Our Father in heaven, Hallowed be Your name. Your kingdom come. Your will be done on earth as it is in heaven.

15

We have a choice to make. Will we serve God or money, God or success, God or ourselves? It is impossible for there to be a tie for first place in our lives. We will know the winner by who or what gets most of our time, attention, devotion, and loyalty. Will the God who gives us money for all of our needs and wants, the One who gives us our gifts and talents to be successful, and the One who created life win, or will it be the things He has given us? We cannot create, provide, or give life in our own power? So why not serve someone who can and let everything else take second place? When we properly assign the roles in our lives we will see that it was always a bad matchup. Nothing compares to God, and He deserves first place.

Challenge

Today challenge yourself to examine what is getting the majority of your time, energy, and love and see if that person or thing deserves it. Then adjust your #1 spot accordingly.

Matthew 6:24 (MSG)

"You can't worship two gods at once. Loving one god, you'll end up hating the other. Adoration of one feeds contempt for the other. You can't worship God and Money both.

16

Relationships, like other things, go through seasons. We have people who have been in our lives for years and others who have been around for only a short time. Just like other things in our lives, some relationships need examination and adjusting. There are times when one person will contribute more to the friendship than others based on the season of the relationship, and there are times when it is an equal exchange. We must look at our relationships as a whole based on the fruit it yields. Questions that we must answer honestly with ourselves are, "Is it an asset or an expense? Does it, overall, yield good fruit or bad fruit? Is this relationship toxic to the health of my soul or does it cause me to be better?" When we are honest with ourselves about the people in our lives, it will make it easier to adjust those particular relationships if necessary.

Challenge

Today challenge yourself to look beyond how

long you've known a person, their feelings, and people's opinions. Evaluate the relationship from an honest place and adjust accordingly.

Matthew 7:20
Therefore by their fruits you will know them.

17

The foundation of any structure is important. It's what stabilizes, holds things together, and is used to build other things on top of. What we choose to use as the foundation to build our empire on will determine its longevity and viability. The success of our family, businesses, or education cannot be built in our own strength, but must be completely reliant on God's strength; leaning on His wisdom and not our own understanding. Anything that we do in our own power has the potential to be destroyed at the slightest bit of adversity. It is unstable. It's time for us to sure up our foundation; submitting each corner, each brick, each nail to the Lord. Let's not labor in vain. Let's build so that it lasts.

Challenge

Today challenge yourself to build on purpose. Ask Him to evaluate the foundation you built on your own; fortify the parts that are stable just lacking His touch, and give Him permission to redo the areas that are subject to fall at any moment.

Matthew 7:26-27

"But everyone who hears these sayings of Mine, and does not do them, will be like a foolish man who built his house on the sand: and the rain descended, the floods came, and the winds blew and beat on that house; and it fell. And great was its fall."

18

Let's not be discouraged if all the good that we are doing is not received well by others all the time. There will be times when we will want to help our family and friends but they do not perceive our help as being help. They may view it as us trying to change them or make them conform to a way of life that they do not want. Change cannot be forced. Some people are not ready to change; it is not convenient for them. It has to be welcomed, accepted and embraced. If people do not receive our help we must accept that it is ok, knowing that we had good intentions and did what we felt was right in our heart. Just consider it a seed sown in their life to be watered by someone else at a later time.

Challenge

Today challenge yourself to keep sowing seeds of help; love beyond the rejection and to try not to take it personally.

Matthew 8:34

And behold, the whole city came out to meet Jesus. And when they saw Him, they begged Him to depart from their region.

19

There will be times when a request is made of you from people who you know do not like you and mean you no good. In fact, they may even have a campaign out against you and go out of their way to discredit you, make you look bad, and try to persuade others to join their "team". These are people who you may feel have no right to ask anything of you, but in these instances you must oblige. For the sake of your integrity and overall peace, you must grant their request. As hard as it may be, you have to be the bigger person during these times and treat them like Christ treated those who He knew for certain were 'anti-Jesus'- merciful, forgiving, loving, peaceful, and gracious.

Challenge

Today, challenge yourself to not automatically reject the requests made by your enemy. Show them the love and compassion of Christ.

Matthew 8:31-32

So the demons begged Him, saying, "If You cast us out, permit us to go away into the herd of swine." And He said to them, "Go." So when they had come out, they went into the herd of swine...

20

It's time to start peeling back and dealing with the layers of the person you have become by default. Past seasons have left you broken, and you have learned to function with this disability. You didn't mean to become bitter and angry. You didn't start out a skeptic and pessimist. You never had trust issues, but somewhere on this journey you were hurt, let down, and disappointed, and at that point you began to change in subtle ways; so subtle that you didn't even notice it. Now you look in the mirror and don't recognize the person looking back at you. You are not happy with you and you don't know why or how you got to this place. The good news is that today is a great day to start over. It's a new day, and you don't have to be the person that you don't want to be. Today you can make a change.

Challenge

Today challenge yourself to view the world through the untainted eyes of the person that you desire to be; give people a fair chance; see the good before you see the bad; trust before you disqualify. Be the you that you want to be.

Matthew 9:16-17

No one puts a piece of unshrunk cloth on an old garment; for the patch pulls away from the garment, and the tear is made worse. Nor do they put new wine into old wineskins, or else the wineskins break, the wine is spilled, and the wineskins are ruined. But they put new wine into new wineskins, and both are preserved."

21

You Are Not Forgotten
Rhoda Turner

Are there times in your life when you feel alone or that God has forgotten about you and your circumstances? **Be not dismayed or deceived God has not forgotten you.** He is there walking with you as you walk through your situation. The enemy wants you to feel alone, forgotten and pushed aside, but you are important and God cares. As God's children, sometimes we can forget about casting our cares on Him. That's what He wants us to do. **He wants us to cast our cares on Him, and then take it a step further and forget about them.**

If someone gives you a gift and holds on to the other end, have they actually given it to you fully? No. It is not yours until they have let it go, and it is in your possession 100%. That's how we do God with our cares, when what He wants is for us to release it to Him and let it go. God wants us to release it, know that He has it, and He's concerned about you.

Matt 6:30-34 says, "Now if God so clothes the grass of the field, which today is, and tomorrow is thrown into the oven, will He not much more clothe you, O you of little faith? "Therefore do not worry, saying, 'What shall we eat?' or 'What shall we drink?' or 'What shall we wear?' For after all these things the Gentiles seek. For your heavenly Father knows that you need all these things. But seek first the kingdom of God and His righteousness, and all these things shall be added to you. Therefore do not worry about tomorrow, for tomorrow will worry about its own things. Sufficient for the day is its own trouble."

Be assured that if God is concerned about the simple things of life than certainly He has your "bigger" problems on His mind as well.

So I encourage you to cast your cares, forget about them, stand in confidence that God has them, and then watch God work it out for you.

22

Foundations
Naomi Grant

"Therefore whoever hears these sayings of Mine, and does them, I will liken him to a wise man who built his house on the rock: and the rain descended, the floods came, and the winds blew and beat on that house; and it did not fall, for it was founded on the rock. But everyone who hears these sayings of Mine, and does not do them, will be like a foolish man who built his house on the sand: and the rain descended, the floods came, and the winds blew and beat on that house; and it fell. And great was its fall. (Matthew 7:24-28)

The durability of a building is dependent on its foundation and is later tested by wear and tear and sometimes the storms it must endure. Likewise **our foundation determines our ability to withstand the storms of life**. Consistent reading of God's word, fervent prayer and a life of worship fortifies the foundation of our heart and cultivates an environment to hear clearly when the voice of God speaks; unless we hear clearly we cannot respond in obedience.

Being in the position to hear is important. Sometimes our storm is so loud that we cannot see the miracle before us, let alone hear the details of our assignment or see the miracle behind our obedience. It is through the storm that those around us can see our lives change thus bringing God glory through every correct response.

In contrast **when we are disobedient we are motivated by what satisfies our emotions**. We often find ourselves being tossed to and fro by the winds of our emotional distress becoming bitter, disenfranchised, confused, angry, most often un-fulfilled, and looking for someone else's assignment.

We must know that the storm has a purpose in our assignment. Embrace your assignment and follow through. You just might like what you look like and appreciate the storm in its passing.

Prayer:
Father, I repent for not being obedient to your instructions. I accept my assignment and embrace my storm. I thank you for being my strong foundation. I am confident as I hear You and obey Your voice, no matter how difficult the storms get, with Your help I can overcome. I thank you that obedience leads to inner strength, outward endurance, and is upheld by Your wisdom. In Jesus' name, Amen.

23

Sometimes you just have to talk to yourself! No matter what the situation looks like and no matter what other people are saying about your situation, there will be those moments when you have to say to yourself, "I am better than this". "This thing won't beat me". "I am who my Daddy says I am." Your circumstance may give you a visual of a defeated you, a sick you, or a depressed you, but you know better than that. You are fearfully and wonderfully made. You are healed and whole. Your sins are forgiven. You are worth it. Voices that say otherwise are just distractions to keep you from seeing you the way your Father sees you, and to keep you from going after greatness.

Challenge

Today challenge yourself to talk to yourself! Remind yourself that you are healed. Tell yourself how wonderful you are. Speak highly of yourself to yourself and drown out the noise of the world.

Matthew 9:21-22

For she said to herself, "If only I may touch His garment, I shall be made well." But Jesus turned around, and when He saw her He said, "Be of good cheer, daughter; your faith has made you well." And the woman was made well from that hour.

24

When we were called by Jesus to follow Him, we weren't just called so that we could be good people and live a nice life. We were given a God-given ability to change lives. There is a time to sit at the Master's feet to learn from Him, but then there comes a time when He sends us out into places that need what we have received while being with Him; a chance for change. The great part about being sent out by Jesus is that He equips us to do the work. He doesn't leave it to us to have to figure out. He gives us the power to speak into the lives of hurting people and to pray for the sick and see results. He empowers us for the assignment.

Challenge

Today challenge yourself to say "yes" to be sent out. Leave your comfortable spot at the feet of Jesus, and go do the work He told you to do.

Matthew 10:1 (MSG)

The prayer was no sooner prayed than it was answered. Jesus called twelve of his followers and sent them into the ripe fields. He gave them power to kick out the evil spirits and to tenderly care for the bruised and hurt lives.

25

No matter what you do people will always have something to say. If you are excelling they may call you a show off. If you make a mistake they may call you a screw up. Don't let the opinions of others define who you are and shape the person you are becoming. Only you and the Lord know the condition and intent of your heart displayed through your actions. Stay in your lane, and do what you are supposed to be doing. Do not try and prove or disprove the words of others. Just do what you know that you are supposed to do and let the Lord's approval be all that counts.

Challenge

Today challenge yourself to stay focused, not entertaining the comments of others. Let people say what they want because they are going to do it whether you want them to or not.

Matthew 11:18-19 (MSG)

John came fasting and they called him crazy. I came feasting and they called me a lush, a friend of the riffraff. Opinion polls don't count for much, do they? The proof of the pudding is in the eating."

26

It is time to take a step back and evaluate the load you are carrying. When the Lord gives you an assignment it comes with grace and peace. It is surrounded by provision and is resourced by heaven. He makes a way for you to successfully do what He has asked of you. If your health has been challenged because of the assignment, if there is no peace, if you are not sleeping, or if your relationships are all strained then it might be time to rethink it all. Is it something the Lord asked of you or something man has asked? The answer makes a big difference.

Challenge
Today challenge yourself to only carry what the Lord gives you. Release everything else into His hands.

Matthew 11:30
For My yoke is easy and My burden is light."

27

In different environments we will undoubtedly find people who may not be for us and/or may not be our biggest fans. When we learn of their dislike we have two choices: engage them or stay away from them. For the sake of peace we should feel free to stay away and give ourselves freely to those who accept us, to those who receive us for who we are, and to those who we are sent to be around. There is no need to stay around people who mean us no good when there is a circle of people who want us around, enjoy our company, and value what we bring to the table.

Challenge

Today challenge yourself to evaluate your social and professional circles. When you find the unwelcomed spot just walk away. You don't have to make a big deal of it. Just get up and go. Do not stay where you are not wanted.

Matthew 12:14-15

Then the Pharisees went out and plotted against Him, how they might destroy Him. But when Jesus knew it, He withdrew from there...

28

It's time to decide and commit. Are we going to produce good fruit or bad fruit? Are we going to speak life into our situation or death? Are we going to walk in integrity or always have an excuse for our bad behavior? A decision has to be made on who we want to be and how we want to live our lives; and then a commitment to that choice has to follow that decision. Whatever it is that we choose to do we should put our all into it, not wavering back and forth.

Challenge
Today challenge yourself to do an inventory of the things you say and do, evaluating if it is overwhelmingly good or bad, then adjust accordingly.

Matthew 12:33-34
"Either make the tree good and its fruit good, or else make the tree bad and its fruit bad; for a tree is known by its fruit. Brood of vipers!

How can you, being evil, speak good things? For out of the abundance of the heart the mouth speaks.

29

Your heart and mouth are connected. If you don't like what is coming out of your mouth then it is time to change what's in your heart. You will speak what your heart authorizes. If the majority of your conversation is laced with sarcasm, pessimistic statements, doubt, or criticism than chances are your heart is full of those same things. The more you say something, the more you hear it. The more you hear it the more you believe it. The more you believe it the more you say it. The cycle repeats itself over and over. If you want things to change you have to change the cycle. Start saying something different until your heart believes it and becomes full of what you want.

Challenge

Today challenge yourself to take a step back and do an unbiased heart check. If there are things that you want to change, let today be the start of that transformation.

Matthew 12:34b NIV

For the mouth speaks what the heart is full of.

30

Do you know that the Lord trusts you so much that He has given you access to information that He has not given to others? A better question would be do you know why you have been given this privilege, why the Lord would trust you with such precious and top secret information? It is because you are ready. You have a heart that is open and is turned to Him. You have proven to Him that you can handle what is revealed to you. Not everyone can be trusted with God's secrets, but you can.

Challenge

Today challenge yourself to keep your eyes and ears open. Be ready at all times for the new information that the Father is ready to tell you.

Matthew 13:10-11 (MSG)

The disciples came up and asked, "Why do you tell stories?" He replied, "You've been given insight into God's kingdom. You know how it works. Not everybody has this gift, this insight; it hasn't been given to them. Whenever someone has a ready heart for this, the insights and understandings flow freely.

31

The Ground is Breaking
Julianna Morlet

There is something new around the corner. Something is about to burst open in this world. The rumble beneath the earth is the sound of evil scrambling; fighting harder to stay prevalent, relevant. But it will not prevail.

We have a promise from the One who has yet to break a single promise that even the fiery gates of hell itself cannot eliminate.

"...This is the rock on which I will put together my church, a church so expansive with energy that not even the gates of hell will be able to keep it out. And that's not all. You will have complete and free access to God's kingdom, keys to open any and every door: no more barriers between heaven and earth, earth and heaven. A yes on earth is yes in heaven. A no on earth is no in heaven." - Matthew 16:18-19 (MSG)

Meaning, there is nothing that will keep the movement of the Spirit, through the vehicle of the Church, from churning faster and faster and faster.

Restoration is God's plan. Redemption. Salvation will be had for the earth and those who dwell in it.
Something is coming.
Something is awakening.

The ground is breaking and light is bursting forth, even brighter today than it was yesterday.

Look for it and I promise you will find it.

32

Pray For Those Who Persecute You
Jessica Koulianos

"But I say to you, love your enemies, bless those who curse you, do good to those who hate you, and pray for those who spitefully use you and persecute you, that you may be sons of your Father in heaven"

Matthew 5:44-45 is a scripture that we have all heard many times in our life, but how many of us have actually done it? I have dealt with many people in my life that have wronged me and hurt me deeply. The flawed girl in me would love to hate them and see them in pain for how they treated me.

There was a time that I was feeling hurt and angry for what someone had done to me, and I was reminded of this scripture. So **I decided to put this scripture to the test.** At first it felt fake and unnatural to pray for someone I disliked so much, but the more I prayed for them, the better I felt. In time my hatred for them was gone. **I began to see them through God's eyes and began to have mercy and compassion on them. I was able to forgive them and move on.**

Now that doesn't mean that I didn't separate myself from those who hurt me, but I began to see how wrong un-forgiveness and hate are, and how they aren't of God.

When you apply this principle of Scripture to your life the Lord does a work in your heart so that you can be free; even if those that have wronged you never change. You are responsible for your heart and your actions. How God deals with them has nothing to do with us. I have seen that when you pray for those that persecute you, your life is blessed in ways that you never imagined.

I challenge you today to search your heart and get alone with the Lord. Pray for those who have hurt you. Call them out by name and really pray for them from your heart. Pray that the lord will help them and change them. Pray for their needs to be met. Pray that the Lord will change the way they are and bless them.

It will feel very weird at first, but keep praying for them. Do it as long as it takes for you to feel free; released from any hurt in your heart towards them.

You will be surprised what God does in you when you apply Matthew 5:44-45 in your life.

33

People are watching us. Our coworkers, our employees, our students, our family members, they are all watching the things we say, how we carry ourselves, and how we treat others. They have taken notes of our consistent behavior of love and loyalty. They notice our smile every day and our pleasant demeanor. They take inventory of our encouraging words, and because they are aware of these things they also notice when things seem off or uncharacteristic of our normal behavior.

Challenge
Today challenge yourself to be mindful of your consistent behavior asking yourself "is this what I want people to remember me by?", and if not then make any necessary adjustments.

Matthew 13:27
So the servants of the owner came and said to

him, 'Sir, did you not sow good seed in your field? How then does it have tares?'

34

We may never know the long term impact that our smile, encouraging words, hugs or pat on the back may have on someone. The truth is that we do these things as a natural part of who we are. At times it's so natural that we don't really even consider the other person at all. But to the person on the receiving side of your kindness it may make all the difference in the world; it could change the tone of their whole day.

Challenge

Today challenge yourself to intentionally sow kindness into someone's life knowing that your seed will result in an incredible harvest.

Matthew 13:31-32

Another parable He put forth to them, saying: "The kingdom of heaven is like a mustard seed, which a man took and sowed in his field, which indeed is the least of all the seeds; but when it is grown it is greater than the herbs

and becomes a tree, so that the birds of the air
come and nest in its branches."

35

What do you place value on and how much is it worth to you? You will know what you place high value on when you can live without everything else and have only that. If your prized possession is your family will you give up your career for it? Will you forgo traveling and extra spending to save for a home? Is life experience more valuable to you than the college experience? The value of something or someone will become very clear to you when you are forced to choose between it and something else that you want.

Challenge

Today challenge yourself to think about what you can and cannot live without and decide if it is worth it.

Matthew 13:45-46 (MSG)

"Or, God's kingdom is like a jewel merchant

on the hunt for excellent pearls. Finding one that is flawless, he immediately sells everything and buys it.

36

There will be times when we desperately want to be by ourselves. We have given and given of our time and energy to others, and now all we desire is a moment for ourselves to process all that has happened, but because of the compassion that we have for others in need, we choose to sacrifice what we rightfully deserve in order to help them. It's in these moments that we realize that others need us more than we need us. We are stronger than we think. We are built to last longer than we imagined. It's in those moments that we see what we are made of. Do we retreat or do we catch a second wind and look at the greater good we could be doing? The more we help others the greater our compassion grows when we see a need. The greater our compassion grows, the more we help. It's a cycle that fuels itself and fuels us to keep going even when we want a break.

Challenge

Today challenge yourself to push beyond what you think are your natural limitations and in order to help someone in need and stretch your compassion to the next level.

Matthew 14:13-14

When Jesus heard it, He departed from there by boat to a deserted place by Himself. But when the multitudes heard it, they followed Him on foot from the cities. And when Jesus went out He saw a great multitude; and He was moved with compassion for them, and healed their sick.

37

What you have will never be enough and will always be enough at the same time. There are times when you may look at what you have (your gifts and talents) and think it is insufficient. When looking at the big picture it may seem insignificant, but do not be discouraged. When you submit all you have to the Lord it will be more than enough to bless not only you and your house, but it will be a blessing to the masses. What you think and view as small the Lord will bless and multiply it to meet the needs of you, your family, your friends, and strangers.

Challenge

Today, challenge yourself to submit what you have to the Lord. Give Him the "ok" to use your voice, your writings, your art work, and watch how many lives, including yours, will be impacted.

Matthew 14:17-20

And they said to Him, "We have here only five loaves and two fish." He said, "Bring them here to Me." Then He commanded the multitudes to sit down on the grass. And He took the five loaves and the two fish, and looking up to heaven, He blessed and broke and gave the loaves to the disciples; and the disciples gave to the multitudes. So they all ate and were filled, and they took up twelve baskets full of the fragments that remained.

38

You have to know Him for yourself. There are times when the things that others have told you about Christ will suffice, but then there are times when only a personal revelation will do; something birthed out of your walk and talk with the Lord (relationship). This personal revelation will not only give you a different perspective and insight of the Lord, but it will teach you so much about yourself. A revelation of who He is will unlock the truth about who you are.

Challenge
Today challenge yourself to spend a few extra minutes with Him cultivating your relationship. Learn more about Him and more about you.

Matthew 16:16-19
Simon Peter answered and said, "You are the Christ, the Son of the living God." Jesus answered and said to him, "Blessed are you,

Simon Bar-Jonah, for flesh and blood has not revealed this to you, but My Father who is in heaven. And I also say to you that you are Peter, and on this rock I will build My church, and the gates of Hades shall not prevail against it. And I will give you the keys of the kingdom of heaven, and whatever you bind on earth will be bound in heaven, and whatever you loose on earth will be loosed in heaven."

39

What do you do when you have done all that you know to do; you have sought counsel and asked for help and nothing has changed for you? You keep pushing. You keep moving forward. You stay persistent. You don't stop until you see a change. There will be times when a setback comes and wants to knock you down, but you have to remain strong and focused on what you want. You will get your desired results if you keep going until you get the right answer from the right person.

Challenge
Today challenge yourself to not give up until you are satisfied with the results of your pursuit.

Matthew 17:15-18 NIV
"Lord, have mercy on my son," he said. "He has seizures and is suffering greatly. He often falls into the fire or into the water. I brought him to your disciples, but they could not heal him."..."Bring the boy here to me." Jesus

rebuked the demon, and it came out of the boy, and he was healed at that moment.

40

Once we get into a routine our day-to-day life does not take much to maintain. We know who to call at what time, which bus to take, and which prayer to pray when someone asks; but what happens when what we've been doing doesn't seem to be effective? There will be instances where a greater effort is required of us in order to get the job done; when we have to take what we have already been doing and add to it. It may require us to call more to check on family members, or get to work earlier to finish the project. We may even have to pray differently. Some things will only change with a greater effort made.

Challenge
Today challenge yourself to evaluate what's working for you and what's not and then try to put forth a greater effort to see things change.

Matthew 17:19-21
Then the disciples came to Jesus privately and

said, "Why could we not cast it out?" So Jesus said to them, "Because of your unbelief; for assuredly, I say to you, if you have faith as a mustard seed, you will say to this mountain, 'Move from here to there,' and it will move; and nothing will be impossible for you. However, this kind does not go out except by prayer and fasting."

41

Shrewd and Innocent at the Same Time
Lauralyn Vasquez

"...Therefore be as shrewd as snakes and as innocent as doves." Matthew 10:16 (NIV)

A while back our family of five went out on a walk with our dog. We were walking on a dirt road with no homes for about a half a mile. One of our daughters, age 10, was up in front with our little dog. In the middle of the road was a coiled up snake that we did not see. The snake completely blended into the dirt road and rocks. In one frightful moment our daughter picked up her dog and ran out of range of the snake. It was a miracle that neither she nor the dog was bitten. We all shook and walked in silence back home as we realized how close our girl was to being bit. Her first thought was to protect her dog and then run.

So what does this have to do with Jesus telling his disciples as they went out to "be as shrewd as snakes and as innocent as doves?" **So often in our eagerness to share the gospel we do everything but be shrewd.** Snakes survive and are successful because they blend in. They wait for the perfect time to strike. We as Christ followers, who want to tell everyone about Christ, can have a tendency to forget that we are to be shrewd. **Being shrewd is about blending into the landscape, becoming unknown and then as the opportunity arises we share the gospel.**

How can you blend in and plan when you are going to share? You do this with gentleness like a dove. Being shrewd is about purpose. We are to share the hope of Christ. That is what Christ sent His disciples to do. **It's not just about blending in either. It's about finding the opportunity to share and taking it with gentleness.** The snakes know they are snakes and it's what they are to do. Doves are naturally harmless and gentle.

How are you as shrewd as a snake and as innocent as a dove? **Challenge yourself to explore your shrewd, snake-like side and your innocent, dove-like side, and seize**

every opportunity presented to you to share the Gospel.

42

Walking in Love
Rhoda Turner

The Bible speaks of three types of love: the love of God for man, man's love for God, and love between mankind. God's loves for man gives us a guideline on how we should love Him and one another.

In Matthew 22: 34-40 "the Pharisees gathered together. Then one of them, a lawyer asked Him a question, testing Him, and saying, "Teacher, which is the great commandment in the law?" Jesus said to him, "You shall love the Lord your God with all your heart, with all your soul, and with all your mind. This is the first and greatest commandment. And the second is like it: You shall love your neighbor as yourself. On these two commandments hang all the Law and the Prophets."

That's what God requires us to do; just that we walk in love. God loved us enough to allow his son to die on the cross for our sins so that we could live life more abundantly. **Sometimes it is hard to show love to others when we don't quite know how to love ourselves.** Know that when you were created it was done in God's image and likeness. **When God made you He took his time. He did not just throw something together.** You were crafted. He knew exactly what He was doing.

I challenge you to work on walking in love, starting with yourself. As you learn to love yourself it becomes easier to love others. When your husband is acting out of character, instead of giving him a piece of your mind, **WALK IN LOVE!** When your child is working on that reserved nerve, instead of getting frustrated and yelling at them, **WALK IN LOVE!** When your boss is blaming you for everything, instead of cursing him or her out, **WALK IN LOVE!** When the cashier at the drive-thru window has an attitude and doesn't want to be at work, instead of giving her the same attitude back, **WALK IN LOVE!**

Remember walking in love is the great commandment. You may be the only love of Christ that is shown to that individual. We are examples of Christ and our lives are testaments of Him.

43

It is inevitable that offenses will come. It is what we choose to do with that offense that will make all the difference. Offense undealt with will fester on the inside like a poison to your body. It will breed resentment, hatred, and disdain. It will alter your mood and your attitude especially in the presence of the one that hurt you. Offense must be addressed in order to preserve the essence of who you are. The end result may or may not be a lifetime friendship, but you will have put yourself in a position to move forward by doing so.

Challenge

Today, challenge yourself to address the issues that may be uncomfortable to deal with. Talk through your issues and make it right.

Matthew 18:15 (MSG)

If a fellow believer hurts you, go and tell him— work it out between the two of you. If he listens, you've made a friend.

44

When we try to change our situations in our own strength we quickly find that it is pointless and a waste of our time and energy. In and of ourselves we do not have the ability, power, endurance, or wisdom to effectively change anything, but when we surrender all of what we do have (our willingness) God can turn everything around for us. Without Him enabling us in everything we set out to do, both large and small, we can't do anything at all.

Challenge
Today challenge yourself to take your hands off of things, and let God change it for you.

Matthew 19:25-26
When His disciples heard it, they were greatly astonished, saying, "Who then can be saved?" But Jesus looked at them and said to them, "With men this is impossible, but with God all things are possible."

45

The mark of a GREAT leader is not found in big words, outward appearance, or financial backing, but it is found in our ability to serve those that you lead. What separates a GREAT leader from an ordinary leader is in our willingness to humble ourselves enough to make those who follow us more important than ourselves. People will only be impressed by our big words and leadership "attitude" for a short period of time. What will make them loyal, faithful, and dedicated is how we view them in our heart and treat them with our corresponding actions.

Challenge
Today challenge yourself to lead with humility. Prefer the "follower" over yourself and watch the difference it will make.

Matthew 20:28
"just as the Son of Man did not come to be served, but to serve, and to give His life a

ransom for many."

46

When you know who you are and are aware of your worth then you will not allow your current situation to cause you to feel ashamed. Things may not look the way you picture them in your future. You may be living paycheck to paycheck when you know God has called you to be a financier of the Kingdom. Your family may not be serving God when you know He has called your whole house to be saved, but when you know that these are temporal things that can turn in a moment's time, thus revealing the greatness that you have always known was there, then you can walk through this season with dignity and pride. Having the knowledge that at any given moment everything can shift for you will empower you to remain hopeful when things look different than you think they should.

Challenge

Today challenge yourself to hold your head up high and see yourself in the light of your promise.

Matthew 21:5, Zechariah 9:9

"Tell the daughter of Zion, 'Behold, your King is coming to you, lowly, and sitting on a donkey, a colt, the foal of a donkey.' "

47

What have you allowed to come in and invade your space altering God's original plan for you. Your home was designed to be a place of peace and rest, but somehow has turned into a place of chaos and confusion. Your job was intended to be a place for you to use your gifts to generate income and has become a place of competition and gossiping. School was supposed to be for learning and is now a party zone. The original design is what creates an environment for you to prosper. It lays the foundation for everything to build on.

Challenge
Today challenge yourself to rediscover the original plan and then do what is necessary to take your space back.

Matthew 21:12-14 (MSG)
Jesus went straight to the Temple and threw out everyone who had set up shop, buying and selling. He kicked over the tables of loan

sharks and the stalls of dove merchants. He quoted this text: My house was designated a house of prayer; You have made it a hangout for thieves. Now there was room for the blind and crippled to get in. They came to Jesus and he healed them.

48

Love... the governing force behind all we do, the backbone of all decisions, the foundation on which all things are built. Love will not only teach us how to treat others, but it will teach us how to treat ourselves. Love will open the door for right decision making. When we allow love to be the deciding factor on whether or not we do or say something then we are guaranteed a victory. Love will always win if it is used. It is the ultimate trump card. It wins in every situation regardless of what else is going on around it. Love has the ability to change everything every time.

Challenge

Today challenge yourself to let love be the deciding vote. Then watch as the outcomes become favorable each time.

Matthew 22:37-40

Jesus said to him, "'You shall love the Lord your God with all your heart, with all your soul, and with all your mind.' This is the first and great commandment. And the second is like it: 'You shall love your neighbor as yourself.' On these two commandments hang all the Law and the Prophets."

49

There is a saying, "*Do as I say, not as I do*". How often do we say one thing and do something completely different? We allow our circumstances to make us appear untrustworthy. We all drop the ball occasionally; whether it is on purpose or unintentional. The question is not "will we have to go back on our word" because things happen; the question is how often do we do it? Do we exhibit inconsistent behavior more often than not or are we the ones that others know they can trust? Dependability is a desirable character trait that we should strive for daily.

Challenge
Today challenge yourself to let your words and your actions match. Be a good example.

Matthew 23:2-3

…"The scribes and the Pharisees sit in Moses' seat. Therefore whatever they tell you to observe, that observe and do, but do not do according to their works; for they say, and do not do.

50

Trouble doesn't have to last forever. Those things that you are facing and dealing with that seem like the end is nowhere in sight, have an expiration date sooner than you think. It may be hard to see it now because other people have given you their professional and personal opinions. You do not have to wait three months before you can be approved for something. You do not have to wait seven years for it to fall off your credit. You are God's chosen and included in His benefit package for your life are truncated seasons. You do not always have to endure the tough times to the extent that the season dictates in the natural.

Challenge

Today challenge yourself to trust in the timing and the agenda of the Lord, because it looks nothing like man's plans for you.

Matthew 24:21-22 (MSG)

"This is going to be trouble on a scale beyond what the world has ever seen, or will see again. If these days of trouble were left to run their course, nobody would make it. But on account of God's chosen people, the trouble will be cut short."

51

Weeds Expire
Naomi Grant

We can become so busy in life that we wake up one day realizing that we have spent, what seems like an eternity, fighting what we have now become; doing things we said we never would do, becoming the product of your greatest fears; We start talking like our mother, acting like our father, and we are now our worst critic. We spend time recalling instances of pain and or abuse that have left us damaged and empty of principles.

However, in those moments **what we thought was weakness was really just untapped strength-** the ability to handle life's circumstances completely opposite of the view we once held so strongly to. "How did I get here?" "Where does this strength come from?" are the questions that we ask ourselves in an effort to ease the pain and the reality of our current situation.

Self- sabotage often plagues us. We blame ourselves for where we are. We criticize the decisions we made and long for answers amidst the weeds. Yes, weeds, vises that suffocate our dreams and kill our vision. Weeds are the thoughts that remind us of our past; the reminder of our failures.

These weeds can feel like thorns amongst what is supposed to be a bountiful harvest crop, but it is those weeds that show our faithfulness to the cause. They sustain us and help us to grow beyond what is perceived humanely possible.

So now what? **Now that you know the weeds in your garden are there to stay, appreciate them.** Name them like a pet you always wanted. It sounds contradictory and it is. It's called maturation. God allows them to build character, patience, and solidify your trust and faith in Him.

As you mature, you begin to respond in love despite the challenges. **The season will change and what was sent to destroy your garden (the weeds) will begin to separate and**

you will see and experience a bountiful harvest. Those weeds in your life will then meet their fate; never to co-exist again.

I encourage you to identify the weeds in your life, those painful and life altering occurrences, and begin to appreciate them for what they really are. It is the weeds that determine the height of your success and make you stronger than you ever thought possible. Fall in love with the process, for your harvest is nearly here!

Weeds only last until harvest time!

Matthew 13:24-30

Another parable He put forth to them, saying: "The kingdom of heaven is like a man who sowed good seed in his field; but while men slept, his enemy came and sowed tares among the wheat and went his way. But when the grain had sprouted and produced a crop, then the tares also appeared. So the servants of the owner came and said to him, 'Sir, did you not sow good seed in your field? How then does it have tares?' He said to them, 'An enemy has done this.' The servants said to him, 'Do you want us then to go and gather them up?' But he said, 'No, lest while you gather up the tares you also uproot the wheat with them. Let both grow together until the harvest, and at the time of harvest I will say to the reapers, "First gather together the tares and bind them in bundles to burn them, but gather the wheat into my barn."

52

It is important to know when to help and when not to help. There will be times when helping others is a good idea, but then there are times when helping will do more harm than good. In some seasons, people have to figure it out on their own. If you are always giving to others in need out of what you have, there may be instances when it just isn't enough to keep both of you going. In the end you may both become depleted, because you are running off of the same resources. It's ok to be selfish at times. Seek the Lord's counsel on each individual occurrence, asking Him if He wants you to give or hold on to your resources.

Challenge

Today challenge yourself to assess the situation before you help. See if helping is going to hurt or help both you and the other person.

Matthew 25:8-9

And the foolish said to the wise, 'Give us some of your oil, for our lamps are going out.' But the wise answered, saying, 'No, lest there should not be enough for us and you; but go rather to those who sell, and buy for yourselves.'

53

Going through the process, walking from season to season, may be difficult at times. We sow seeds and then sit back waiting for the harvest. We have endured the hard times, put time in on our knees in prayer, and done what we could with what we had. Now what? Now we wait with anticipation of what's to come. Our faithfulness over what has been placed in our hands in the last season will not only yield a bountiful harvest, but it will yield "more". In this next season of "more" we will not only experience an increase of natural things, but in both peace and joy.

Challenge

Today challenge yourself to remain faithful and diligent to the end. Your more is coming.

Matthew 25:21

His lord said to him, 'Well done, good and faithful servant; you were faithful over a few things, I will make you ruler over many things. Enter into the joy of your lord.'

54

How are you treating Jesus? How we treat others is a direct reflection on how we treat Jesus. It is so easy to get caught up in the hustle and bustle of our day and ignore the needs of others. Our family and friends require much of our attention, and our jobs have us working late. We become consumed in our own bubble that, at times, it is hard to see that there is a world that needs us. There is a stranger who needs a smile and some kindness, an elderly woman who needs help carrying groceries, and a child who needs encouragement. They are depending on us to make a difference in their day.

Challenge

Today challenge yourself to see beyond your immediate circle and be mindful of how you are treating others. They need you.

Matthew 25:38-40

When did we see You a stranger and take You in, or naked and clothe You? Or when did we see You sick, or in prison, and come to You?' And the King will answer and say to them, 'Assuredly, I say to you, inasmuch as you did it to one of the least of these My brethren, you did it to Me.'

55

There are times when the people who are the closest to you and are connected with your promise will not understand the sacrifices that you will make for the promise. They may even look at what you are giving up and have a better plan that in their eyes would be more effective. Stand your ground. Do what you know to do for your promise; it is yours not theirs. If it means something of significance to you it is going to cost you something, but only you can determine what that cost is going to be. Never let others dictate to you what your promise is worth.

Challenge

Today challenge yourself to think about what your promise means to you, and then go after it with an appropriate sacrifice.

Matthew 26:7-9

A woman came to Him having an alabaster flask of very costly fragrant oil, and she poured it on His head as He sat at the table. But when His disciples saw it, they were indignant, saying, "Why this waste? For this fragrant oil might have been sold for much and given to the poor."

56

Would you do what you do if no one ever knew your name? Would you do what you love to do if you never had a promise of reward? The woman with the alabaster box sacrificed, poured out her love for Jesus from her heart; not looking for anything in return. She wanted to show Jesus what He meant to her, and although He promised, *"What this woman has done will also be told as a memorial to her."* Her name, Mary, is only mentioned once in the Gospels, and twice she is called 'a woman'. Will you be ok if future generations see your wonderful acts and only a few attributed it to you and others call you this man or this woman?

Challenge
Today challenge yourself to think about the motivation behind what you do. Are you

doing it for notoriety or because you love it?

Matthew 26:6-7, 12-13

And when Jesus was in Bethany at the house of Simon the leper, a woman came to Him having an alabaster flask of very costly fragrant oil, and she poured it on His head as He sat at the table...

For in pouring this fragrant oil on My body, she did it for My burial. Assuredly, I say to you, wherever this gospel is preached in the whole world, what this woman has done will also be told as a memorial to her.

* ...a woman came having an alabaster flask... (Mark 14:3)

*Then Mary took a pound of very costly oil of spikenard... (John 12:3)

57

You are worth it. Sometimes people will place value on you or believe in you to a level that you don't feel you deserve. They honor your word as truth, they believe in your dreams, and push you to do. They may give you gifts that, to you and possibly to others around you, seem too much to accept, but you are worth it. They see in you what God sees in you and they have chosen to partner with Him in His vision for your life.

Challenge

Today challenge yourself to believe that you are worth the investment of someone else's time, faith, and resources.

Matthew 26:7-10 NIV

… a woman came to him with an alabaster jar

of very expensive perfume, which she poured on his head as he was reclining at the table. When the disciples saw this, they were indignant. "Why this waste?" they asked. "This perfume could have been sold at a high price and the money given to the poor." Aware of this, Jesus said to them, "Why are you bothering this woman? She has done a beautiful thing to me.

58

You don't know what you are capable of until you do it. It is so important to live a balanced life. We can never lean so far in one direction that, in our own eyes, we think that we are too "good" to do something "bad" or too "bad" to do something "good". What have you told yourself that you would never do and what have you said that you'd never be good enough to do? Dependence on the Lord for wisdom, discernment and grace is vitally important as we encounter each situation. We all have the potential to do great things, make an impact on our society, and influence lives; but because we are humans we are not above giving in to temptation. This is why we must surround ourselves with people who will help us keep a balanced perspective and who will always speak truth to us.

Challenge

Today challenge yourself to be balanced in your view of yourself.

Matthew 26:33-34

Peter answered and said to Him, "Even if all are made to stumble because of You, I will never be made to stumble." Jesus said to him, "Assuredly, I say to you that this night, before the rooster crows, you will deny Me three times."

59

Do you know who you are? Do you know that other people will question your identity just to see if you will confirm or deny their suspicions of you? Everyone sees that within you lies the strength to fight, the faith to believe for the "impossible", and the wisdom to navigate through tough situations. They already know that you possess authority, influence, and the ability to shift an atmosphere with your presence. You are who you are and you cannot deny it. You are a world changer and a history maker. You leave your mark everywhere you go. People will question you to see if you know what they know about you. Don't disappoint them with you answer.

Challenge

Today challenge yourself to respond with confidence about your identity the next time someone asks you who you are.

Matthew 27:11a

Now Jesus stood before the governor. And the governor asked Him, saying, "Are You the King of the Jews?" Jesus said to him, "It is as you say."

60

Do not defend yourself. Your accusers know who you really are and will try desperately to discredit you, make you believe something about you that is not true, or put you in a position where your words will do more harm than good. They are aware of your track record of honesty and integrity. They know that things change for the better when you are around. Your influence is undeniable. Some of their accusations may be true and some may be baseless, have no power, and hold no truth. No matter what, you stand your ground in silence. In time you will be vindicated and all will know the truth.

Challenge

Today challenge yourself to let your defense strategy be silence.

Matthew 27:12

And while He was being accused by the chief priests and elders, He answered nothing.

61

Be encouraged. You are moments away from the greatest season of your life to date. Yes, things are looking dark and bleak. Yes, people are talking about you to your face and behind your back trying to discredit you. Yes, you are tired and it feels like the life is being sucked out of you. BUT do not give up. You are closer than you think to the greatest breakthrough and revealing that you have ever seen. The fulfilment of God's promise to you concerning your future is about to become alive and active. God's promise to your family for them is about to be made known through you. Your new season is going to shift things in your life to such a degree that it will automatically shift the season of those who are associated with you. They will experience the benefits of your faithfulness to your process, your endurance to keep going when things were hard, your determination to go through whatever it takes, and your silence when you had every right to defend yourself. What you have done will affect everyone.

Challenge

Today challenge yourself to finish this season strong. Remain faithful until the very end so that you can enjoy the newness of the next season with no regrets.

Matthew 27:35, 50-53

Then they crucified Him... And Jesus cried out again with a loud voice, and yielded up His spirit. Then, behold, the veil of the temple was torn in two from top to bottom; and the earth quaked, and the rocks were split, and the graves were opened; and many bodies of the saints who had fallen asleep were raised; and coming out of the graves after His resurrection, they went into the holy city and appeared to many.

Matthew 28:6a

He is not here; for He is risen, as He said…

62

People will continue to expect dead things to stay dead and broke things to stay broke when they have no examples of hope to look at.. Sometimes in order for others to believe in the "impossible" they have to know that the reality of an alternative exists. People will remain in a defeated state if they don't hear of the success stories. We have to tell them about our experiences. They may not believe that their hard times will ever end until we share with them about the times when we had to borrow money from family just to make ends meet. They may not believe that their children will ever "learn their lesson" until we share our child's story of going from expulsion to honor roll. They may not believe that they will ever be able to kick an addiction until we share how we overcame something that we never thought we could give up. People need us to embrace our past, share our story and help them. People need us to give them hope.

Challenge

Today challenge yourself to not shy away from sharing your story when the appropriate time presents itself. Give someone hope.

Matthew 28:5-7 NIV

The angel said to the women, "Do not be afraid, for I know that you are looking for Jesus, who was crucified. He is not here; he has risen, just as he said. Come and see the place where he lay. Then go quickly and tell his disciples: 'He has risen from the dead and is going ahead of you into Galilee. There you will see him.' Now I have told you."

NOTES

_____

_____

_____

_____

_____

_____

_____

_____

_____

_____

_____

BRANDIE MANIGAULT

When she learns of something good, her first instinct is to share it with the world; whether it is a sale at a store, a beautiful picture, a good book, or a revelation from the Word of God.

With a Business Degree from Oral Roberts University and a Masters in Human Services/ Marriage and the Family from Liberty University, she has managed both the administration and the finances departments for businesses, ministries, and churches in Maryland, California, and Texas. She has helped local churches build from the ground up and consults for ministries nationwide. She also writes a book review column for Grace and Glory Magazine based out of Maryland. Alongside her husband, Tim, Brandie cofounded Healing Voice Ministries, a nonprofit ministry whose aim is to be a voice of healing and hope provoking the earth to experience fellowship with God through worship all by His grace & love. Together they serve at their local church in California, minister to couples embarking on their journey towards marriage as well as to couples in crisis through marriage coaching, and provide leadership development training. With all that she has going on, her number one priority is her husband Tim and their three children; Sydney, Kristina, and Samuel. Brandie can say with all assurance that there is no other assignment more important, more fulfilling, more challenging or more rewarding than being a wife and mother.

Brandie is a strong believer that "Love Wins"!

CONTRIBUTING WRITERS

Among the many titles **Naomi Grant** wears, none are more fulfilling than the title of wife and mother. Married for 16 years, Naomi and her husband Dwight, live in Nassau Bahamas while pastoring both locally and overseas with New Genesis Bermuda. As a rising voice in the worship community, Naomi will tell you that everything you see on stage first starts with private worship, dedicated time with the Lord, and a heart to please Him.

Jessica Koulianos' heart is to demonstrate the love of Jesus through hands on outreach. She has a burning desire to help those in need; whether it is the homeless, the hungry, the hurting children or the pregnant mother who is afraid and lost. After her love for God, Jessica has a burden for the family unit and introducing families to God's priorities. She also has a prophetic ministry as well as praying for the sick and frequently appears on worldwide television ministering and sharing the love of Jesus.

Julianna Morlet is a worship leader at Shoreline Church in Austin, Texas with her husband, Tyson Morlet and their daughter. If you could have coffee with her, she would tell you the one thing that's proven constant in her life of following of Christ, it is this: "All through the history of mankind God has yet to break a promise and He's not going to start with us." You can read more of her story at her blog juliannamorlet.com or connect with her on social media @juliannamorlet.

Along with her husband, Jason, **Rhoda Turner** is the Co-Pastor of Christian Faith Fellowship Church located in Green Bay, WI. She is a devoted mother of 4 beautiful girls, and is the youngest daughter of 10. She enjoys spending time in the presence of God, singing, spending time with her family, and nurturing and molding one of Gods most precious gifts-children.

Lauralyn Vasquez is a wife of 24 years and a mother of three teenagers. In her home there is always an adventure happening. As a young girl her desire was to share the hope she had found in Jesus Christ. Starting at age 10 she organized her first back yard Bible study and prayed with the neighborhood children. She loves listening to others' stories and pointing them towards the hope and transforming power of Jesus Christ. She holds a BA from Westmont, a certificate in Leadership and Spiritual Direction, and a Masters in Teaching and Learning with technology. Currently she is Small Groups Pastor at Rancho Community Church in Temecula California, encouraging leaders and connecting people in order for their love to abound as they grow in knowledge and insight.

THANK YOU

Thank you to my **Father**, my big brother **Jesus**, and my Help, **Holy Spirit**. Without you nothing is possible, but with you ALL things are.

To my husband, my best friend, my biggest fan. **Tim** there is no one else on this earth that I would rather do "life" with. Thank you for believing in me and pushing me beyond what I thought I could do. **Sydney, Kristina,** and **Samuel**... thank you for keeping me so tired and distracted for a season that it pushed me to want more of Jesus! I love you with all that I have.

Daddy and Ma, Alan and Bettie Jones... the first two members of my fan club! Thank you for championing me in every season and loving me without limitations. **My sister, my Crystal Jones**... Before there was anyone else, there was you and me. Thank you for always being by my side and in my corner.

Deidra Manigault thank you for never being an "in-law", for telling me the truth, and helping me sharpen my gift even when you didn't know that's what you were doing.

To all those who took this journey of New Day Fresh Start with me I am forever grateful. To all the **contributing writers**… thank you for trusting God, for believing in the vision He gave me, and for keeping your ears open to hear from Him what your contribution looked like. **Jackie Epps** and **Siobhan Saulsbury** for being a sounding board for my thoughts and for reading every word to make sure I presented His message with excellence. **Karen Carrozi**, my friend, thank you for allowing the Holy Spirit to speak to you on how He would have this book to look. Your work amazes me. **Dianna Dumas**, thank you for challenging and pushing me and for creating a look that ties everything together perfectly. **Pastor Melva Henderson**… I am honored that you would go on this journey with me. Thank you.

www.ingramcontent.com/pod-product-compliance
Lightning Source LLC
LaVergne TN
LVHW051410080426
835508LV00022B/3015